I Wish I Could Dine With A Porcupine

Poems by Brian Moses
Illustrations by Kelly Waldek

Fife COUNCIL

Wayland

Fife Council Education Department
King's Road Primary School
King's Crescent, Rosyth KY11 2RS

Hodder Wayland Paperback Poetry

The Boneyard Rap And Other Poems by Wes Magee

The Upside Down Frown Collected by Andrew Fusek Peters

The Worst Class In School Collected by Brian Moses

I WISH I COULD DINE WITH A
PORCUPINE
© Hodder Wayland 2000
Text © Brian Moses 2000

Prepared for Hodder Wayland by
Mason Editorial Services
Designer: Tim Mayer

Published in 2000 by
Hodder Wayland, an imprint of
Hodder Children's Books
Reprinted in 2004
A Catalogue record for this book is available from
the British Library.

ISBN 0 7502 2856 3

Printed in Hong Kong

Hodder Children's Books
A division of Hodder Headline Ltd.
338 Euston Road, London NW1 3BH

CONTENTS

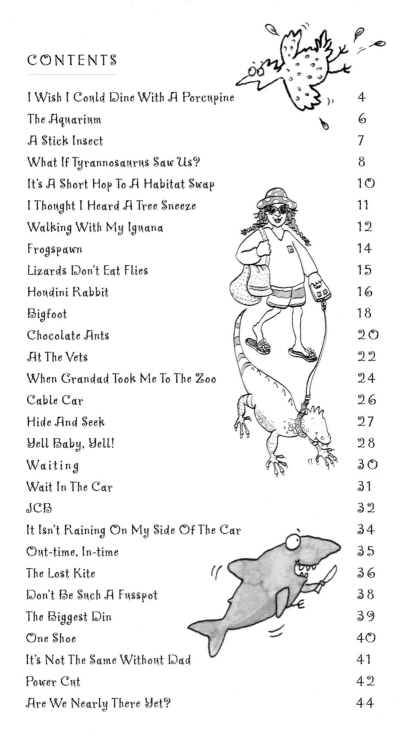

I WISH I COULD DINE WITH A PORCUPINE

I wish I could dine with a porcupine
or take afternoon tea with a whale.
I wish I could race with a cheetah
or visit the house of a snail.

I wish I could chat with a bat
and learn about its habits.
I wish I could dig a deep burrow
and spend the day with rabbits.

I wish I could fly balloons with baboons
or watch jellyfish eating jelly.
I wish I could perfume spray a skunk
so he wouldn't be quite so smelly.

I wish I could learn about a worm
as I slide along on my tummy,
or meet a baby hippo
and his hippopotamummy.

I wish I could feast with a wildebeast
or rescue a mule from his load.
I wish I could bake a cake with a snake
or hop down the road with a toad.

I wish I could take all these creatures
for a holiday by the sea,
we'd have our own beach barbecue
and toast marshmallows for tea.

THE AQUARIUM

The aquarium
was disappointing:

The dogfish
didn't bark,
the jellyfish
didn't wobble.

The sea mouse
didn't squeak,
the starfish
didn't shine.

The hermit crabs
were crabby,
the clams
clammed up,
and the plaice
stayed in one place.

But when the swordfish
attacked us,
and the sharks invited us
to be their lunch. . .

we rode away fast. . .
on a sea horse!

A STICK INSECT

A stick insect
is not a thick insect,
a macho-built-like-a-brick insect,
a brawl-and-break-it-up-quick insect,
not a sleek-and-slippery-slick insect
or a hold-out-your-hand-for-a-lick insect.

No way could you say it's a cuddly pet
or a butterfly that hasn't happened yet.

And it won't come running when you call
or chase about after a ball.
And you can't take it out for a walk
or try to teach it how to talk.

It's a hey-come-and-look-at-this-quick insect,
a how-can-you-tell-if-it's-sick insect,
a don't-mistake-me-for-a-stick

   insect. . .

WHAT IF TYRANNOSAURUS SAW US?

What it Tyrannosaurus saw us
as we went tiptoeing by?
What if he raised his terrible head
and focused his bleary eye?

What if Tyrannosaurus saw us,
licked his teeth and thought, "Here's dinner"?
Could we run and outdistance him
with the speed of an Olympic winner?

We could tell him that we were small fry
and that he'd do better to wait.
Our teacher would be along soon,
she'd be meatier meat for the plate.

But what if Tyrannosaurus saw us
and gave a ROAR that shook the trees?
What if our legs refused to move
and we stumbled and fell to our knees?

One thing we know, he wouldn't bore us
with any social chit-chat.
He'd open his jaws and gobble us both
in fifteen seconds flat!

But what if Tyrannosaurus saw us,
could we offer him our Smarties,
tell him if he were friendlier
he'd be asked to birthday parties?

Tell him if he stopped bullying
and behaved more sensibly,
then we'd invite him and his family
to call at our house for tea.

You've heard about changing rooms,
well, why can't animals do it too?
Dolphin swap with eagle,
penguin with kangaroo.

Polar bear offers snow hole,
gorilla quits jungle den,
camel gives up the desert
for a home in a Scottish glen.

Termites leave their mounds
for a coral reef under the sea.
A mole grown tired of a hole
is fixing a nest in a tree.

Badger offers his burrow
to a lobster and a crab,
but who will swap places
with a slug sleeping under a slab,

Or a spider who offers a web
but doesn't say when he's leaving?
Well, it could turn out to be true
but it all takes some believing.

Animals changing habitats –
it might catch on at the zoo,
every year, when spring comes round,
old homes being swapped for new.

I thought I heard a tree sneeze!
I'm not really surprised,
standing out there in all weathers,
damp feet, a cloak of wet leaves.
Is it any wonder they catch cold?

I wouldn't be pleased
to be a tree, couldn't nip out
for cough sweets or a quick vapour rub
down my bark.
I'd be left all night in the dark,
feeling shivery, feeling cold.

I thought I heard a tree sneeze,
but perhaps I was mistaken.
What do you think?

11

WALKING WITH MY IGUANA

(Words in brackets to be repeated by another voice or voices)

I'm walking (I'm walking)
With my iguana (with my iguana)

I'm walking (I'm walking)
With my iguana (with my iguana)

When the temperature rises
to above eighty-five,
my iguana is looking
like he's coming alive.

So we make it to the beach,
my iguana and me,
then he sits on my shoulder
as we stroll by the sea. . .

and I'm walking (I'm walking)
With my iguana (with my iguana)

I'm walking (I'm walking)
With my iguana (with my iguana)

Well if anyone sees us
we're a big surprise,
my iguana and me
on our daily exercise,

till somebody phones
the local police
and says I have an alligator
tied to a leash.

When I'm walking (I'm walking)
With my iguana (with my iguana)

I'm walking (I'm walking)
With my iguana (with my iguana)

It's the spines on his back
that make him look grim,
but he just loves to be tickled
under his chin.

And I know that my iguana
is ready for bed
when he puts on his pyjamas
and lays down his sleepy (Yawn) head.

And I'm walking (I'm walking)
With my iguana (with my iguana)

Still walking (I'm walking)
With my iguana (with my iguana)

With my iguanaaaa...................

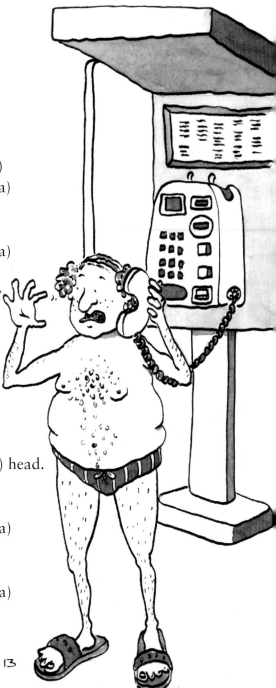

13

FROGSPAWN

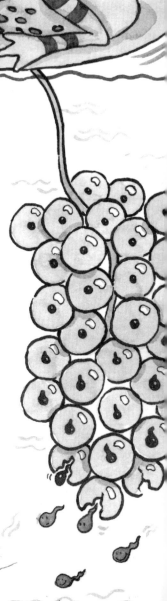

All those commas
waiting to be born
out of frogspawn.

All those wrigglers
waiting to wriggle.

All those dots
about to hop.

Watch them quiver
slide and slither.

A city afloat
of musical notes

that wriggle away
from the bars of a song.

"We won't be long"
they sing.

There's an odd little fact
about lizards
that not many people know –
they can't stand flies
and they'd rather eat fries.
So they wait around at
takeaways,
hoping there might be
throwaways
left in the bag
when somebody bins it.

Yes, lizards hate flies
and would rather eat fries
anyday

(especially with vinegar!).

HOUDINI RABBIT

He'll lead you round the garden
in a funny old dance,
then just when you think
you're in with a chance
he'll pause while he munches
some radish tops,
you make a grab
but away he hops,

Houdini, Houdini rabbit,
Houdini, Houdini rabbit.

And on that rabbit face
I'm sure I see a smile,
"I'll let you catch me,
but not for a while,
not until I've had a really long run,
not until I've made you SHOUT.
I love playing chasing games with you
when I have the chance to come out."

Houdini, Houdini rabbit,
Houdini, Houdini rabbit.

There are holes in progress
all across the lawn,
when I catch you rabbit
you'll wish you weren't born.
Next thing I know I'm down in the mud,
you can see that this pleases Houdini,
he's off down the path, tail in the air,
Just wait till I get my hands on you,
you MEANIE !

Houdini, Houdini rabbit,
You meanie, Houdini rabbit,
Houdini.

17

Our house is full of Bigfoot
or should that be Bigfeet?
We watched them from our window
as they stumbled down the street.

They knocked upon our door
and asked to come inside.
"Don't leave us here," they pleaded,
"We need a place to hide."

Now there's Bigfeet in the kitchen
and Biggerfeet in the hall.
On a patch of grass in our garden,
Bigfeet are playing football.

There's Bigfeet in our garage
and Bigfeet in the shed,
while underneath the duvet,
Bigfeet sleep in my bed.

18

Bigfeet lounge in the lounge
all watching our TV.
There's nowhere much to sit
since they've broken our settee.

Some Bigfoot put his foot
right through our bedroom ceiling.
The darkness in our loft, he said,
was really quite appealing.

The airing cupboard Bigfoot
keeps our water hot.
"No problem at all," he says,
"I like this job a lot."

They make an awful racket
up and down our stairs,
they queue to use the bathroom
and block the sink with hairs.

At night they growl and snore,
loud as a thunderstorm,
but all these fur coats everywhere
keep us cosy and warm!

CHOCOLATE ANTS

If they started to sell
chocolate-covered ants
at the superstore
would you buy them?

If they gave them away
in a tasting test
would you try them?

If they said these are yummy,
and good for you too,
they keep away colds
and protect you from flu.

Would you say
you can give me
a packet or two.

And if you liked them
maybe you'd try. . .

aniseed fleas
and jelly slugs,
sugar-coated earwigs
or peppermint bugs

a range of tastes
waiting for you,
try 'Eleph - ants"
for a jumbo chew.

but I'd say no way –
I just couldn't,
could you?

AT THE VETS

When we took our dog to the vets
we sat and waited with all kinds of pets.

There were hamsters with headaches
and fish with the flu,
there were rats and bats
and a lame kangaroo.

There were porcupines
with spines that were bent
and a poodle that must have been
sprinkled with scent.

There were dogs that were feeling
terribly grumpy
and monkeys with mumps looking
awfully lumpy.

There were rabbits with rashes
and foxes with fleas,
there were thin mice in need of
a large wedge of cheese.

There were cats complaining
of painful sore throats,
there were gerbils and geese
and two travel-sick goats.

There were two chimpanzees
who both had toothache,
and the thought of the vet
made everyone
s...h...a...k...e...

When Grandad took me to the zoo,
Grandma said:
"You make sure he behaves himself. . ."
But he didn't.

He made faces at the monkeys,
he poked a penguin with his stick.
He went far too close to the tigers
and he woke up an angry snake.

He called the hippos names,
he dropped ice cream down his shirt.
He queued to go on the slide
till a zookeeper sent him out.

Then as we left he said,
"We'll come back as soon as we can."

"Sorry Grandad," I answered,
"Next time I'm coming with Gran!"

CABLE CAR

Over the mountains
we love to float
in our cable car
like a giant swing boat.
On the valley floor
far down below,
monopoly houses,
row upon row.

Inside a cloud
we disappear,
someone screams
but there's nothing to fear,
and very soon
we're at the top,
we never wanted
this journey to stop.

Maybe someday
somebody will
build a cable car
up the steepest hill
on and on
till it reaches the stars,
cable car travel
all the way to Mars.

Hide and seek
all down the street,
behind parked cars,
look out for their feet.
Inside a dustbin
– ugh, you stink!
Stupid place to hide,
I just didn't think.
Crouch down behind walls
in someone's front yard –
my knees are hurting,
this concrete's hard.
I know that they'll find me,
they always do,
I wish I could find
somewhere good, like you.
But something happens
to give me away,
a dog starts barking
or I hear someone say:
"Hey you by the fence,
get away from there."
So I give myself up,
it just isn't fair.
I dream that I'll find
somewhere perfect one day
and I'll hide there forever
till they all go away.

YELL BABY, YELL!

It was coming through loud and clear,
from the baby's room right down to my ear,
a glorious noise, a tremendous din,
like someone scraping a violin.

yow-ow-ow-ow-ow-ow-ow-ow-owl!

I was really amazed, I just didn't dream
that something so small could holler and scream
like Pavarotti on a chewed-up tape
when she opens her mouth and lets it escape.

yow-ow-ow-ow-ow-ow-ow-ow-ow-owl!

I ran to the garden, I wanted to hide
but I even heard Radio Baby outside,
and I had to admit it, I was really impressed,
on any noise-o-meter she'd be the best

yow-ow-ow-ow-ow-ow-ow-ow-ow-owl!

Now if anyone calls they don't stay very long,
even our cat has packed up and gone,
The neighbours can't sleep, they look dreadfully pale
and I hear that they're putting their house up for sale.

yow-ow-ow-ow-ow-ow-ow-ow-ow-owl!

WAITING

My mum hasn't come
and I'm left standing
all on my own –
what should I do?

She said she'd be here,
said she wouldn't
be late, she'd be
leaving work at two.

Plenty of time to get the bus
and pick me up from school,

but everyone else has gone home
and I'm waiting here, feeling a fool.

And I'm biting my lip
to keep from crying,
she'll be here soon
I hear myself lying. . .

But what if something's happened,
what if something's wrong?
She's never been this late before,
she's never made me wait this l

o

n

g.

When Mum says, "Wait in the car,
I'll only be gone a minute,"
she's always longer.
We read or play games
and then start to worry.
Perhaps she's run away for good,
she always said she would
if we didn't behave.
Perhaps she's been kidnapped
by bank robbers and bundled into
their getaway car.
Perhaps she's been run over
by a steamroller,
or hypnotised by a magician,
or savaged by a pack
of hungry pekingese.
Perhaps she's picked a fight
with a Sumo wrestler!

And when she does come back
it's always, "Sorry kids,
but I met an old friend
and we had such a lot to talk about,"
or, "I just popped into that shop
as they had a sale on. . ."
And we hide our yawns
and think how boring
our Mum is.

I'm in love with a JCB,
it's huge, it's greedy and it eats messily,
gulping up great gobfuls of food
then spitting them out, mum calls that rude!

I watch it all day as it lumbers about
while the men stand round it and signal or shout:
"More over here Jack, get stuck in. . ."
And the engine cranks up a dreadful din.

The head swings round to look at me
like some dinosaur from prehistory.
Its jaws snap shut like a terrible trap
but the man in the cab never gets in a flap.

He sits there calmly turning the wheel,
throwing levers, how does it feel
to be in control of such a beast
as each day it scoffs its enormous feast?

Oh I'm in love with a JCB,
but I don't think that it's in love with me!
It turns its head and looks my way,
it opens its mouth as if to say:

"Better scoot before I grab you,
better scram before I nab you. . ."
I don't like the look that it's giving me,
I'm not in love with a JCB
         after all!

IT ISN'T RAINING ON MY SIDE OF THE CAR.

It isn't raining on my side of the car,
and I don't want to sit inside now we've travelled this far.
Please let me out, unlock the door,
there's a whole new beach for me to explore,
and it isn't raining on my side of the car.

On the side I'm on the sky is turning blue,
I can see a rainbow, the sun is shining through.
Let's go outside and start to play,
we've already wasted half the day,
and it isn't raining on my side of the car.

OUT-TIME, IN-TIME

Out-time, out-time,
run around and shout time,
shake it all about time,
out-time, out-time.

In-time, in-time,
did you lose or win time,
chuck it in the bin time,
in-time, in-time.

Out-time, out-time,
have a knock about time,
give your friend a clout time,
out-time, out-time.

In-time, in-time,
it's time to begin time,
stop the noisy din time,
in-time, in-time.

THE LOST KITE

Our kite was a magic bird
  and the wind took it into the sky,
    above our heads, above the trees,
    flying way up high.

    But the wind was a thief
    who wanted our kite,
    it tugged and tugged
  with all of its might.

And the wind was a blade
  that could cut anything.
    It took our kite
    and left us with the string.

    We watched it twist and dive,
      we heard it flutter and swish.
    We felt it flap and fall
  and wriggle like a fish.

  Then it took our kite again
  and raced it up a hill,
it tied the string around
    the sails of an old windmill.

    The kite broke free once more,
    into the path of a plane.
    It looked as if our kite
  might be travelling to Spain.

Our kite was caught again
in the branches of a tree,
but the wind blew long and hard
until the kite broke free.

*We watched it twist and dive,
we heard it flutter and swish.
We felt it flap and fall
and wriggle like a fish.*

Next it found a church
and twisted round the spire,
then flipped across the street
to hook on telephone wire.

Then the wind gave a mighty blow
and we lost sight of our kite,
we were looking for it everywhere
while the day ran out of light.

And as we stared from our window
to see the face of the moon,
we wondered if our kite
might be passing by there soon.

*We watched it twist and dive,
we heard it flutter and swish.
We felt it flap and fall
and wriggle like a fish.*

And we both remember that kite,
we know we always will.
In some distant magical place
it's sure to be flying still.

Don't be such a fusspot,
an always-in-a-rushpot.

Don't be such a weepypot,
a sneak-to-mum-and-be-creepypot.

Don't be such a muddlepot,
a double-dose-of-troublepot.

Don't be such a wigglepot,
a sit-on-your-seat-don't squigglepot.

Don't be such a muckypot,
a pick-up-slugs-and-be-yuckypot.

Don't be such a sleepypot,
a beneath-the-bedclothes-peepypot.

Don't be such a fiddlepot,
a mess-about-and-meddlepot.

Don't be such a bossypot,
a saucypot, a gigglepot,
don't be such a lazypot,
a nigglepot, a slackpot.

And don't call me a crackpot. . .
Who do you think you are?

Let's see who can make
the biggest din?
That's me, I said,
with my violin.

I'll scrape the strings,
I'll screech and I'll wail
like a dog when someone
treads on his tail.

No me, I said
with my kettle drum,
I'll thump and thump
till I upset Mum.

No me, I said
I can make a din,
so I opened my mouth
and began to sing,

It was awful!

One shoe by the roadside,
who on earth is careless enough
to lose one shoe?
Surely you'd notice if you hobbled home
on one shoe?
Surely you'd think it was odd?
Some do-gooder would shout out –
"Where's your other shoe then?"
Some busybody would comment –
"That's a strange way to walk!"
You'd be the talk of the town,
one shoe off, one on,
one foot up, one down.
And how could you ever replace
your lost shoe?
Have you ever tried going into a shoe shop
and saying, "I'll just take one please."
Shoes come in pairs, like socks,
you don't find one shoe shops.
So if you're careless and lose one shoe,
best lose the other one too.

I always sat on his knee
for the scary bits when we watched TV,
my head tucked into his chest,
Mum always fidgets, Dad was best

And it's not the same without Dad.

He piggy-backed me up the stairs,
pulled sticky bubblegum out of my hair,
didn't tell Mum when he should have done
when Dad played around it was really fun.

And it's not the same without Dad.

We fed the ducks down at the park,
he held me when I was scared of the dark
he didn't mind if I got things wrong,
when I felt weak, he was sure to be strong.

But everything's changed now he's gone.

POWER CUT

A storm swaggered out of the night
like an evil creature looking for a fight.
It wrapped its arms around our home
and spoke with a low and frightful moan.

Mum got up at half past three,
went downstairs and made cups of tea.
Soon after that the lights went out.
"Mum, come quick," I heard myself shout.

"I don't like it Mum, everything's gone black,
what's happened, are we under attack?"
"Don't worry," she said, "There'll be light again soon,
I'll bring you a candle to brighten your room."

But at breakfast time there was still no power,
the house grew colder with each passing hour.
We had to have bread instead of toast,
we wouldn't be cooking our Sunday roast.

I couldn't play tapes or watch TV
there was no hot water for making tea.
When we opened up the freezer door,
melted ice cream dripped on the floor.

We ate our tea by candlelight,
and carried our candles to bed that night.
Dad said we'd be back to normal soon
as I fell asleep by the light of the moon.

It's a long way to drive to our holiday home
so we set off early.
We stop at the end of our street
and my sister says:
"Are we nearly there yet?"

Dad grins, mum smiles,
"No darling", she says. "It's a long way yet."
And we move out into the slow flow of traffic.

Ten minutes later we've left the town behind
and we're out on the open road,
and my sister says:
"Are we nearly there yet?"

"No", snaps Dad.
"It's a long way to go yet.
Read a book, play a game, have a drink."

Ten minutes later my sister says,
"There. That was a good book that was.
Are we nearly there yet?"

Dad raises his eyes towards the sky.
Mum pats my sister's hand, "No darling,
it's still a long way to go, have another drink,
then why don't you have a snooze?"

My sister closes her eyes.
Five minutes later she stretches, yawns,
"I've had a lovely sleep," she says,
"Are we nearly there yet?"

"If you say that one more time," says Dad,
"I'll stop the car, turn it round
and we'll all go home. Do you understand?"

Mum gives my sister a sticker book
that she's been saving for emergencies.

My sister sticks her stickers in all the wrong places,
FINISHED! she yells.
Dad's face looks grim.
"Are we. . ."
"DON'T SAY THAT AGAIN," says Dad.

"Why don't you sing us some songs," says Mum,
"Read another book, play I-spy, have another drink."

My sister does really well this time.
Half an hour goes by.
Then we get stuck behind some tractor
on the road to the motorway.
"Are we nearly there yet?"

Dad stops the car.
He gets out, he does a war dance,
he kicks the car tyres.
He goes round to my sister's side of the car,
opens the door and shoves his face up
very close to hers.
Then he doesn't say anything.
He just glares.

He closes the door, gets back into the car
and drives off once more.

My sister looks at me.
I put a finger to my lips.
"Are we nearly there yet?" she whispers.

Mum turns round, hands out toffees, fruit.
"Have another drink," she says.

Ten minutes later my sister says. . .

Well, actually she doesn't, she says,
"Can we stop somewhere quick,
I'm really bustin'."

MORE POETRY FROM HODDER WAYLAND

Hodder Wayland Poetry Collections:
Themed anthologies illustrated by Kelly Waldek.
270 x 220 mm, full-colour, 32 pages: £9.99 hb/ £4.99 pb

Poems About Animals
Poems About Festivals
Poems About Food

Poems About Seasons
Poems About Space
Poems About School

Poems About Me/Poems About You and Me:
Poetry about what it means to be a member of society.
270 x 220 mm, full-colour, 32 pages: £9.50 hb/£4.99 pb
Also available as big books/educational packs
Big Books 440 x 360mm, £13.99

The Worst Class In School
With illustrations by Kelly Waldek. A special collection of
poems selected and commissioned by Brian Moses follows the
worst class in school through a chaotic museum visit,
shambolic school photo, disastrous encounter with the dinner
lady and a trip to the zoo that defies description.
204 x 145mm, black & white, 48 pages: £3.99 pb only

The Boneyard Rap and Other Poems
With illustrations by Keith Brumpton. A whole host of spooky characters come to life
in the poems of Wes Magee – meet Pauline Poltergeist, the ghosts of The Grange,
young Jocelyn Joakes, Acker Abercrombie and the rest of the ghostly gang.
204 x 145mm, black & white, 48 pages, £4.50 pb only

Poems About:
Themed collections of poems for primary
children with full-colour photographs.
*27 x 22 cm, full-colour, £4.99
paperback only*

Poems About Families
Poems About Feelings
Poems About Journeys
Poems About Weather

TO ORDER

Contact Hodder
Wayland's Customer
Services Department on:
01235 400414,

or write to them at:
39 Milton Park,
Abingdon, Oxon, OX10
4TD, UK